Consultant, Istar Schwager, holds a Ph.D. in educational psychology
and a master's degree in early childhood education.
She has been an advisor, consultant, and content designer for numerous parenting,
child development, and early learning programs including the *Sesame Street*
television show and magazines.
She has been a consultant for several Fortune 500 companies
and has regularly published articles for parents
on a range of topics.

Louis Weber, C.E.O.
Publications International, Ltd.
7373 North Cicero Avenue
Lincolnwood, Illinois 60646

Permission is never granted
for commercial purposes.

Manufactured in the U.S.A.

8 7 6 5 4 3 2 1

ISBN 1-56173-484-5

active minds

opposites

PHOTOGRAPHY
George Siede and Donna Preis

CONSULTANT
Istar Schwager, Ph.D.

Publications
International,
Ltd.

on

On and off,
a puppy's
new bed.

off

off

Off and on,
a hat on
your head.

on

in

In and out,
   a truck dumping rocks.

out

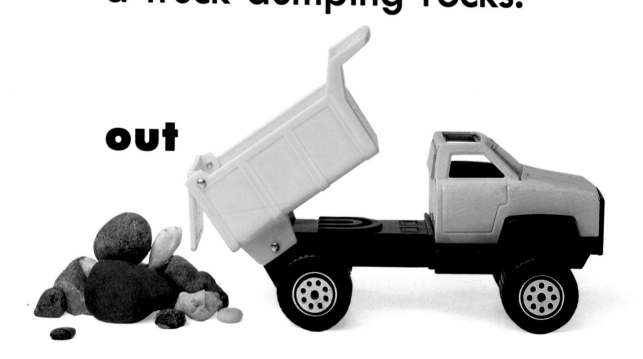

Out and in,
a jack-in-the-box.

out

in

front

back

Front and back,
a fire fighter's hat.

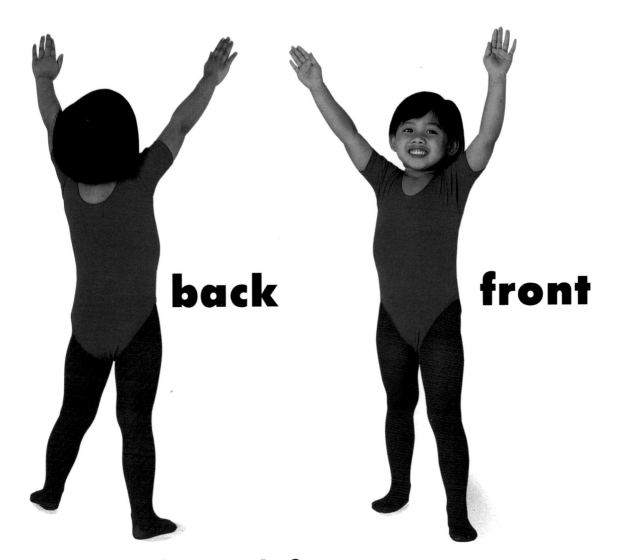

back   **front**

Back and front,
a young acrobat.

open

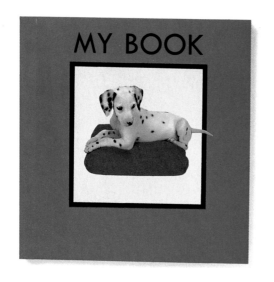

Open and closed, a picture book.

closed

Closed and
open,
let's take
a look.

open

up

Up and down,
touch your
toes.

down

up

Down and up,
bounce it
goes!

down

Stop and go,
around the town.

stop

go

go

Go and stop,
now sit down.

stop

big

Big and little,
a dog and
a pup.

little

little

Little and big,
a balloon
blown up.

big

over

Over and under,
two bears are
at play.

under

over

under

Under and over,
two trains on
their way.